The stories at this level

There are very few words in these s
pictures as in the text. The simple te
the characters who live in West Street. Your children will probably
remember the words very quickly, although they will not be sounding
them out letter by letter. This is fine: recognising and remembering words
are very important skills in early reading.

Before you start reading with your children, read the story and activities
first yourself, so that you become familiar with the text and the best way
to give it expression and emphasis when reading it aloud.

Always sit comfortably with your child, so that both of you can see the
book easily.

Read the story to your child, making it sound as interesting as possible.
Add comments on the story and the pictures if you wish. Encourage your
child to participate actively in the reading, to turn over the pages and to
become involved in the story and characters. Even though children can't
read, they enjoy guessing what is going to happen from the pictures, and
talking about the emotions of the story.

This may be enough for one sitting, but don't give your child the idea that
the book is finished with. Encourage your child to take the book away and
to look through it alone, to find any bits that either of you particularly
enjoyed.

Next time you look at the book with your child, suggest "Let's read the
story together. You join in with me." The text in the speech bubbles is often
the same as the text at the bottom of the page, so one of you can read the
text in the bubbles, and one can read the text at the bottom of the page.
This time follow the words with your finger under them as you read.
Don't stop to repeat words; keep the interest up and the story line
flowing along.

Now ask your child, "Do you want to read the story to me this time?"
If your child would like to do this, join in where necessary if help is
needed. The timing of this stage will depend on your child's readiness

to take over. Do not rush! Try to avoid the idea that reading is a great race where you are always urging children on to harder and harder text.

The activities at this level

The activities at the back of the book need not be completed at once. They are not a test, but will help your child to remember the words and stories and to develop further the skills required for becoming a fluent reader.

The activities are often divided into three parts.

One part is designed to encourage you both to talk about the stories, to predict what will happen and to recall the main events of the story.

One part encourages children to look back through the book to find general or specific things in the text or the pictures. Your child learns to begin to look at the text itself, and to recognise some individual words and letters. Don't press on with these activities too quickly; your child may need to wait a bit before tackling them. Children's general understanding of a story often comes before their ability to make distinctions between individual words and letters.

One part suggests drawing or writing activities which will help your children feel they are contributing actively to the story in the book.

When you and your child have finished all the activities, read the story together again before you move on to another book. Your child should now feel secure with it and enjoy being able to read the story to you.

Tamla's animals

by Helen Arnold

Illustrated by Tony Kenyon
and Frances Thatcher

A Piccolo Original
In association with Macmillan Education

Look at my animals.

This is my lion.

A lion.

This is my monkey.

A monkey.

This is my elephant.

This is my elephant.

An elephant.

This is my giraffe.

A giraffe.

This is my zebra.

23

A lion and a monkey
and an elephant and
a giraffe and . . .
a zebra!

Wake up, Anna.

Time for tea.

Looking at the pictures and words with your children

1. Let's look at Tamla's toy animals.

Can you find the page which shows all her toys?
   How many toy animals can you see?
   What animals are they?

What's the name of the animal with a long neck?
   Can you find the word for it in the story?

What's the name of the animal with the stripes on its coat?
   Can you find the word for it in the story?

Which animal has a long nose?
   Can you find the word for it in the story?

Which animal is very fierce?
   Can you find the word for it in the story?

Which animal have we missed out?
   Can you find the word for it in the story?

2. Anna is thinking about the real animals which are like the toy ones.

Can you remember what the real lion was doing in the story? Can you find the picture to see if you are right?

Now ask your child the same questions about the monkey, giraffe and elephant.

3. Let's look at some letters.

Which animal's name begins with this letter?   e

Which animal's name begins with this letter?   z

Which animal's name begins with this letter?   m

Which animal's name begins with this letter?   g

Which animal's name begins with this letter?   l

Things for your child to do

1. Ask your child to draw the lion, elephant, zebra, monkey and giraffe. Can they copy the name of each animal under each drawing?

lion   elephant   zebra

monkey   giraffe

2. Say to your child: "I'll tell you a story like the one in the book. When I stop, you guess what word I'm going to say next."

Once upon a time there were five animals in the jungle. One was very fierce and had sharp _____. The other animals were afraid of him. He was a _____.
One had tusks and a very long _____. He liked to stand in a pool and spray water on his _____ to keep cool. He was an _____.
Another animal got his food from the leaves on the top of a high _____. He could do this because he had a long _____. He was a _____.
One animal sat in a tree and ate a _____. He was a _____.
The last animal had a coat with black and white _____. He was a _____.

3. Give your child five pieces of paper.
Write at the bottom of each page one of the five phrases below.
Print them in the same style as in the book.
As you print them, read the phrases to your child.
Then jumble up the pages.
Ask your child to draw an appropriate picture above each phrase.
Only read the phrase again if your child asks you to.

monkey in the tree

elephant in the water

zebra with stripes

giraffe eating leaves

lion roaring

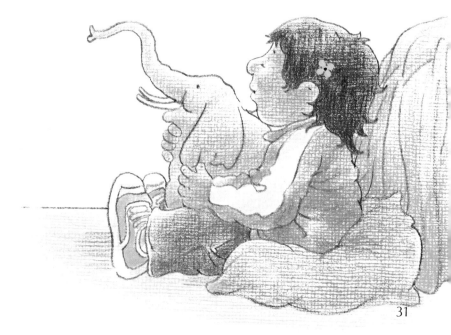

These activities and skills:	will help your children to:
Looking and remembering	hold a story in their heads, retell it in their own words.
Listening, being able to tell the difference between sounds	remember sounds in words and link spoken words with the words they see in print.
Naming things and using different words to explain or retell events	recognise different words in print, build their vocabulary and guess at the meaning of words.
Matching, seeing patterns, similarities and differences	recognise letters, see patterns within words, use patterns to read 'new' words and split long words into syllables.
Knowing the grammatical patterns of spoken language	guess the word-order in reading.
Anticipating what is likely to happen next in a story	guess what the next sentence or event is likely to be about.
Colouring, getting control of pencils and pens, copying and spelling	produce their own writing, which will help them to understand the way English is written.
Understanding new experiences by linking them to what they already know	read with understanding and think about what they have read.
Understanding their own feelings and those of others	enjoy and respond to stories and identify with the characters.

First published 1988 by Pan Books Ltd, Cavaye Place, London SW10 9PG

9 8 7 6 5 4 3 2 1

Editorial consultant: Donna Bailey

© Pan Books Ltd and Macmillan Publishers Ltd 1988. Text © Helen Arnold 1988

British Library Cataloguing in Publication Data
Arnold, Helen
Tamla's animals. — (Read together. Level 1).
I. Title II. Series
428.6   PE1119
ISBN 0-330-30213-2

Printed in Hong Kong